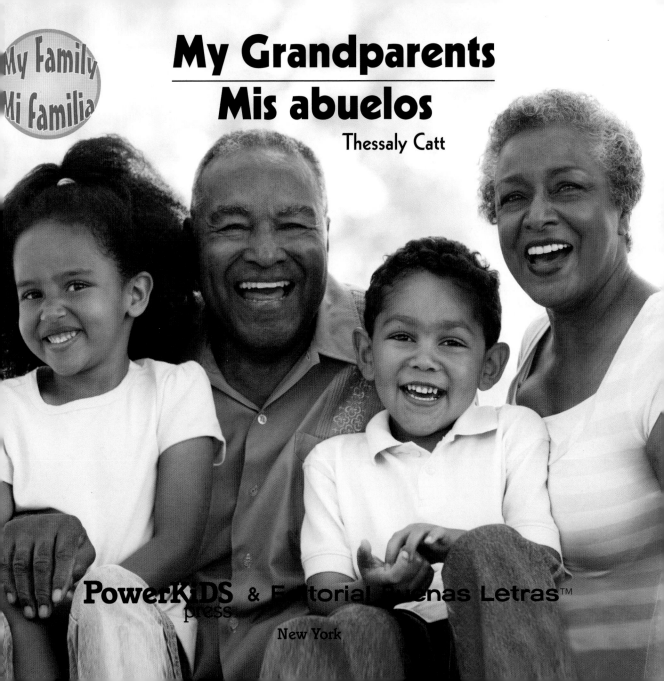

My Family
Mi familia

My Grandparents
Mis abuelos

Thessaly Catt

PowerKiDS press & Editorial Buenas Letras™

New York

To Nan and Pop, otherwise known as Mom and Dad

Published in 2011 by The Rosen Publishing Group, Inc.
29 East 21st Street, New York, NY 10010

First Edition

Editor: Maggie Murphy
Book Design: Ashley Burrell

Photo Researcher: Jessica Gerweck
Spanish Translation: Eduardo Alamán

Photo Credits: Cover, pp. 5, 7 (dad, grandfather right, grandmother right, mom), 11, 12–13, 22–23 Shutterstock.com; p. 7 (grandfather left) © www.iStockphoto.com/Juanmonino; p. 7 (grandmother left) © www.iStockphoto.com/Elena Ray; p. 7 (brother) © www.iStockphoto.com/Ekaterina Monakhova; p. 7 (sister) © www.iStockphoto.com/quavondo; p. 8 © www.iStockphoto.com/Andres Balcazar; p. 14–15 Getty Images; p. 17 © Jose Luis Pelaez/age fotostock; p. 18–19 © www.iStockphoto.com/digitalskillet; p. 20 James Day/Getty Images.

Library of Congress Cataloging-in-Publication Data

Catt, Thessaly.
  My grandparents = Mis abuelos / Thessaly Catt. — 1st ed.
    p. cm. — (My family = Mi familia)
  English and Spanish.
  Includes index.
  ISBN 978-1-4488-0716-1 (library binding)
  1. Grandparents—Juvenile literature. 2. Grandparent and child—Juvenile literature. I. Title. II. Title: Mis abuelos.
  HQ759.9.C38 2011b
  306.874'5—dc22

                              2010007492

Manufactured in the United States of America

CPSIA Compliance Information: Batch #WS10PK: For Further Information contact Rosen Publishing, New York, New York at 1-800-237-9932

Web Sites: Due to the changing nature of Internet links, PowerKids Press and Editorial Buenas Letras have developed an online list of Web sites related to the subject of this book. This site is updated regularly. Please use this link to access the list: www.powerkidslinks.com/family/grand/

Contents / Contenido

Your grandparents are part of your family. Your family is a group of people who love you.

Tus abuelos son parte de tu familia. Tu familia es un grupo de personas que te quieren.

This is a **family tree**. It shows all the members of a family.

Éste es un **árbol genealógico**. Nos muestra a los miembros de una familia.

Family Tree / Árbol Genealógico

Grandfather / Abuelo

Grandmother / Abuela

Grandfather / Abuelo

Grandmother / Abuela

Mom / Mamá

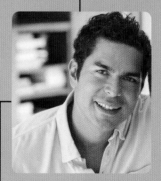

Dad / Papá

Brother / Hermano

Sister / Hermana

Elena calls her grandparents Nan and Pop. What do you call your grandparents?

Elena les dice a sus abuelos, Nan y Pop. ¿Cómo les dices tú a tus abuelos?

Grandparents like to
do many different things.

Los abuelos disfrutan haciendo
muchas cosas distintas.

Mr. and Mrs. Díaz keep in touch with their family online.

Los abuelos Díaz mantienen contacto con su familia usando la computadora.

14

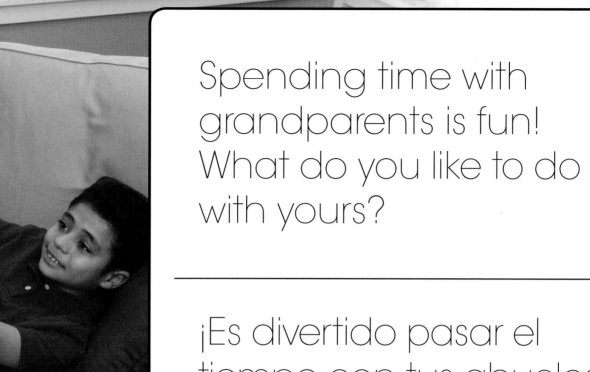

Spending time with grandparents is fun! What do you like to do with yours?

¡Es divertido pasar el tiempo con tus abuelos! A ti, ¿qué te gusta hacer con ellos?

15

Eva's grandmother teaches her about their family.

La abuelita de Eva le habla acerca de su familia.

Every family is different. Ben lives with his grandmother. What is your family like?

Cada familia es diferente. Ben vive con su abuelita. ¿Cómo es tu familia?

19

Families get together for special **events**. Luz's grandparents dance together at parties.

Las familias se reúnen para celebrar **eventos** especiales. Los abuelos de Luz bailan en las fiestas.

Families are very important. They take care of each other.

La familia es importante. En una famila nos cuidamos los unos a los otros.

Words to Know / Palabras que debes saber

events (ih-VENTS) Things that happen, often planned ahead of time.

family tree (FAM-lee TREE) A chart that shows the members of a family.

árbol genealógico (el) Una tabla en la que se muestra a los miembros de una familia.

eventos (los) Sucesos que, a menudo, se planean con anticipación.

24